My Science Library

# Solid or Liquid?

by Amy S. Hansen

Science Content Editor:
Kristi Lew

Rourke
Educational Media

rourkeeducationalmedia.com

Scan for Related Titles
and Teacher Resources

**Science content editor: Kristi Lew**

A former high school teacher with a background in biochemistry and more than 10 years of experience in cytogenetic laboratories, Kristi Lew specializes in taking complex scientific information and making it fun and interesting for scientists and non-scientists alike. She is the author of more than 20 science books for children and teachers.

www.rourkeeducationalmedia.com

Photo credits:
Cover © justin maresch; Cover logo frog © Eric Pohl, test tube © Sergey Lazarev; Page 3 © nikky-tok; Page 5 © Voronin76; Page 7 © oku; Page 9 © travis manley; Page 11 © Valentyn Volkov; Page 13 © Suzanne Tucker; Page 15 © Studio Foxy; Page 17 © Sinisa Botas; Page 19 © Darren Brode; Page 20 © Thomas M Perkins; Page 22 © Sinisa Botas, travis manley, oku; Page 23 © Valentyn Volkov, Studio Foxy, Darren Brode

Editor: Kelli Hicks

Cover and page design by Nicola Stratford, bdpublishing.com

Library of Congress Cataloging-in-Publication Data

Hansen, Amy.
 Solid or liquid? / Amy S. Hansen.
    p. cm. -- (My science library)
 Includes bibliographical references and index.
 ISBN 978-1-61741-726-9 (Hard cover) (alk. paper)
 ISBN 978-1-61741-928-7 (Soft cover)
 1.  Solids--Juvenile literature. 2.  Liquids--Juvenile literature. 3.  Matter--Properties--Juvenile literature. I. Title.
 QC176.3.H36 2011
 531--dc22
                                2011003764

Rourke Educational Media
Printed in the United States of America,
North Mankato, Minnesota

rourkeeducationalmedia.com

customerservice@rourkeeducationalmedia.com  •  PO Box 643328 Vero Beach, Florida 32964

Turn on the tap.

Water runs out. Water is a **liquid**.

5

Liquids are runny. Liquids cannot hold a **shape**.

Liquids need a **container**.

**Pour** a glass of milk. The milk is a liquid.

Sit down. Your chair is hard. It is a **solid**.

13

Solids hold their own shape. They are not runny.

15

You can **break** solids. Each piece holds its shape.

Look at the cookie. You can break it. Each piece holds its shape.

My cookie is a solid. And it is almost gone!

1. Which are runny, liquids or solids?

2. Which can you break, liquids or solids?

3. Is your spoon a solid or a liquid?

# Picture Glossary

**break** (BRAYK):
To make something snap or crack into pieces.

**container** (kuhn-TAY-ner):
An object such as a cup, a bottle, or a box that holds something else.

**liquid** (LIK-wid):
A substance that pours easily.

**pour** (POR):
The action of making a liquid flow freely, usually from one container to another.

**shape** (SHAYP):
The form of an object.

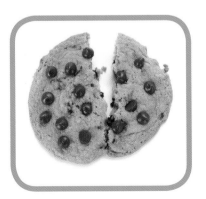

**solid** (SAH-lid):
An object that is firm. It is not a liquid or a gas.

## Index

## Websites

www.strangematterexhibit.com/
www.surfnetkids.com/glacier.htm
www.pbskids.org/zoom/activities/sci/

## About the Author

Amy S. Hansen is a science writer who still enjoys experimenting with solids and liquids, like making bubbles with baking soda and vinegar. She writes about science mysteries and lives in the Washington, D.C. area with her husband, two kids, and two cats.